Science Games & Puzzles

Laurence B. White, Jr.

drawings by
Marc Tolon Brown

Addison-Wesley

To Dave. . .
who guarantees every experiment
because they worked for him

Science Games: text Copyright © 1975 by Laurence B. White, Jr.
Illustrations Copyright © 1975 by Marc Tolon Brown
Science Puzzles: text Copyright © 1975 by Laurence B. White, Jr.
Illustrations Copyright © 1975 by Marc Tolon Brown
All Rights Reserved
Addison-Wesley Publishing Company, Inc.
Reading, Massachusetts 01867
Printed in the United States of America
DEFGHIJK-WZ-89876543

Library of Congress Cataloging in Publication Data

White, Laurence B
  Science games & puzzles

  Originally published as separate volumes entitled
Science games and Science puzzles.
  SUMMARY: Includes simple games, puzzles, and experi-
ments which demonstrate basic scientific principles.
  1. Science — Experiments — Juvenile literature.
2. Scientific recreations — Juvenile literature.
[1. Science — Experiments. 2. Scientific recreations]
I. Brown, Marc Tolon. II. Title.
Q164.W48 1979   507′.2   78-20897
ISBN 0-201-08606-9

Games are to Play

A game is a challenge.
Something to try . . . something to learn . . .
something to be good at.

- Race a drop of water
- Blow the biggest bubble
- Build an eight cup skyscraper

The games in this book work with science!
Science, like a game, is something to try . . .
to learn . . . and be good at.
What a nice way to investigate science . . .
to play science games . . .
by yourself, with friends,
and even with your cat!

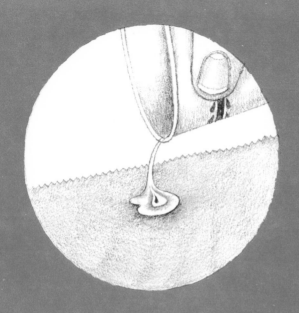

Race with a Drop of Water

Get a big piece of waxed paper.
Lay it flat.
Pour a little water on it.
The water will form a big round drop.
Pick up the paper carefully.
Hold it by both ends.
Tip the paper back and forth.
Make the water drop run around.
How fast can you make it go?
Watch it . . . you may tip a bit too far!

Shadow Game

What is this a shadow of? A dog?
No, it just looks like a dog.
The shadow was really made by a hand.
Shadows are made by blocking out light.
They really are nothing, but they can look like something.
Hold your hands in the sunlight,
or hold your hands between a lamp and a wall.
Can you make shadows that look like these?

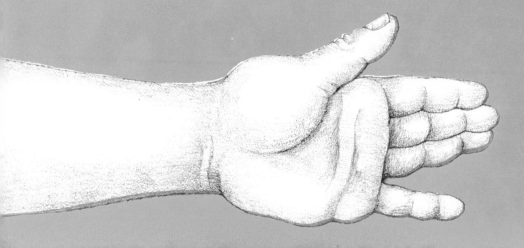

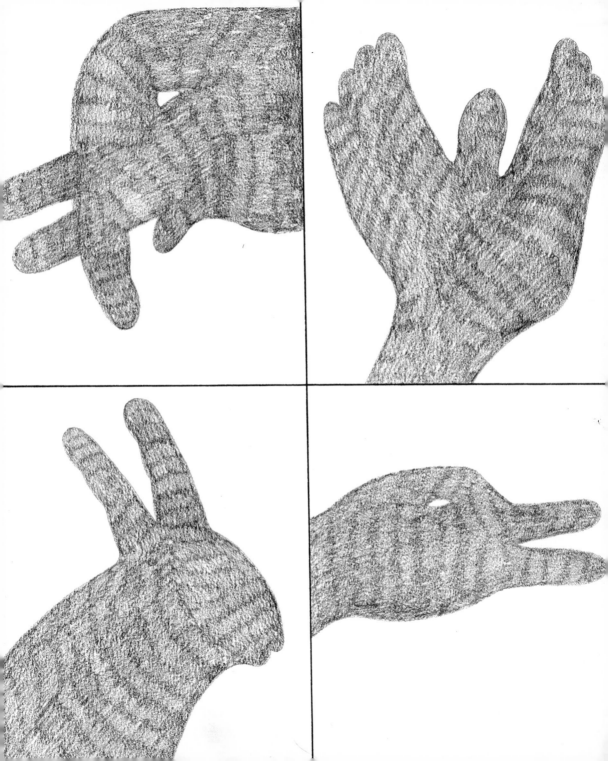

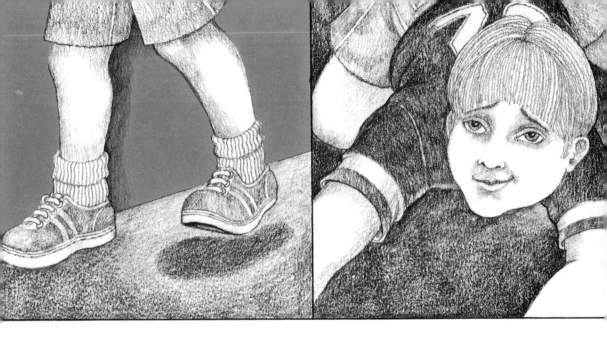

Stand Up, Do Not Fall Down

Sometimes you cannot keep from falling.
Try this. Stand sideways against a wall.
Push the side of your foot against the wall.
Now try to lift your other foot.
It feels like it is stuck to the floor.
The wall stops your body from bending.
If you did lift your foot,
without bending your body,
you would fall down!

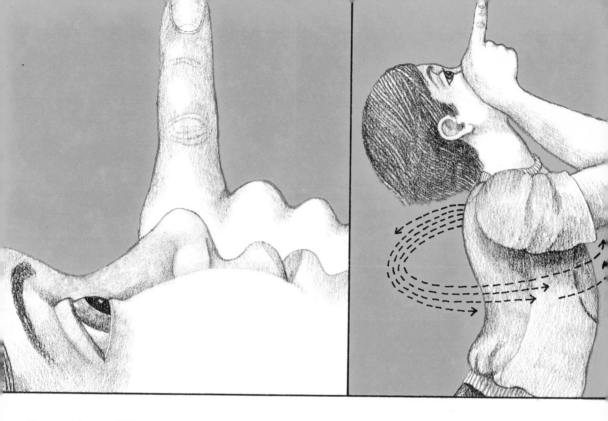

Can You Walk in a Straight Line?

Look up.

Point your finger up from the end of your nose.

Look at the end of your finger.

Keep looking and turn around three times.

Then walk in a straight line.

You try to walk straight,

but you still feel like you are going around.

It will make you very dizzy.

Can You Blow 100 Bubbles?

Can you blow 100 bubbles?

With one breath?

Pour some dishwashing liquid in a cup.

Dip in one end of a drinking straw.

Take it out.

Blow in the other end.

Keep blowing.

You will blow lots of bubbles.

The bubbles will be tiny.

You may even blow 100.

Blow the Biggest Bubble

Who can blow the biggest bubble?
Give everyone a drinking straw.
Use dishwashing liquid for soap.
Dip in the straw and blow gently.
Who blows the biggest bubble?
Try cutting your straw end like a cross.
Now it will hold more soap.
Your bubble will be the biggest.

How High Can You Float a Bubble?

Try this in the winter on a very cold day.
Go outdoors with some bubble soap.
Blow some bubbles.
Your warm breath makes the bubbles very light.
They are much lighter than the cold winter air.
The bubbles will quickly float upwards.
How high?

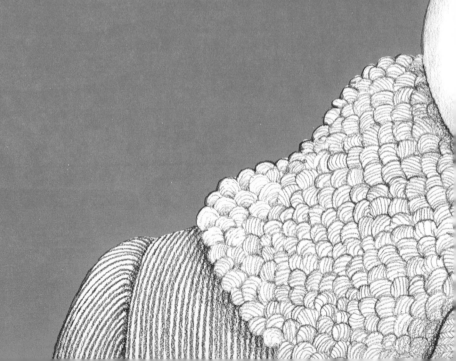

Pencil Pick Up

Lay a pencil in the middle of a table.

Bend down. Look at the pencil level with the tabletop.

Close one eye. Keep it closed.

Quickly reach out and try to pick up the pencil.

You will probably miss it.

It is very hard to do.

Now try it with both eyes open.

It is easy with two eyes helping.

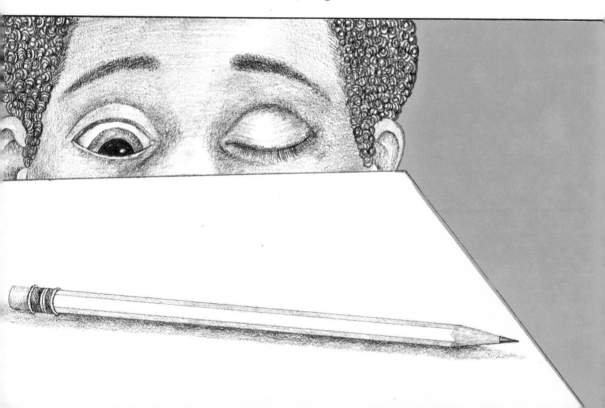

How Hot Can You Make It?

Push a thumbtack into a pencil eraser.

Touch the thumbtack with your lip.

It feels cool.

Rub the tack hard on your sleeve.

Rub hard 20 times.

Touch it to your lips.

It feels warm.

Rubbing makes it hot . . .

The harder you rub . . .

The longer you rub . . .

How hot can you make the thumbtack?

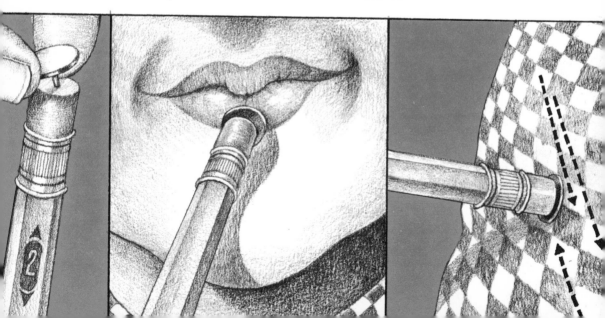

Do Two Things Together

Can you do two things at the same time?
Most people cannot.
Print your name on a piece of paper.
Move your foot in a circle.
Try to do both at the same time.
Why is it hard to do?
Because you have to think
about your hand and foot
doing different things.

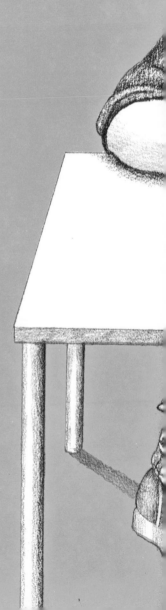

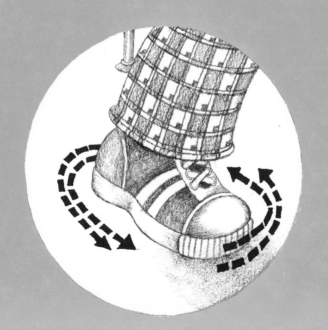

How Cold Can You Make It?

Soak a facecloth in warm water.
Quickly . . . take it outdoors.
Hold it by one corner.
Spin it around and count to ten.
Touch your face with the cloth.
Surprise! It is very cool.
Spinning dries some of the water.
As the water dries, the cloth gets cooler.

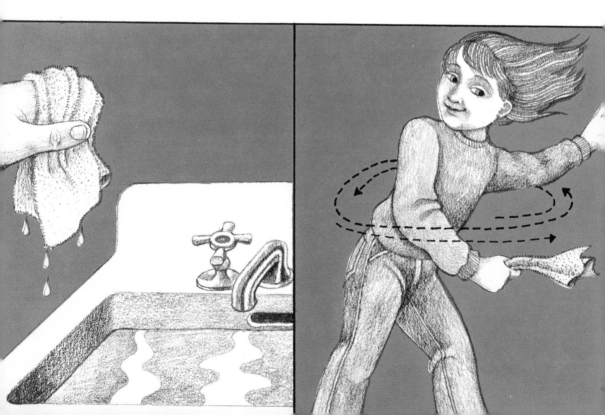

Are You As Long As Your Arms?

Hold your arms and hands out straight.

Have someone cut a string just that long.

Put one end of the string on the floor.

Does the other end reach the top of your head?

Try it with other people.

Are most people as tall as their arms are long?

Penny Dropping

Drop some coins into an empty glass.

Will they always fall into the glass?

Pretty easy, wasn't it?

But, what happens if you put the glass at
the bottom of a bowl of water?

Water slows the coins down.

It pushes the coins aside.

A lot of them miss the glass.

Drink Some Raindrops

Next time it rains
set an empty glass outside.
Catch some raindrops in it.
Raindrops are pure water.
You can drink raindrops.
The water may taste strange.
Most water we drink comes from the ground.

Touch Your Fingers

Hold your arms out straight and
point your fingers.
Then close your eyes.
Try to touch your fingers together.
You can do it if you go slowly.
If you move faster it gets harder.
Now open your eyes and try it.
Much easier, isn't it? Why?
Because our eyes help show
our bodies how to move.

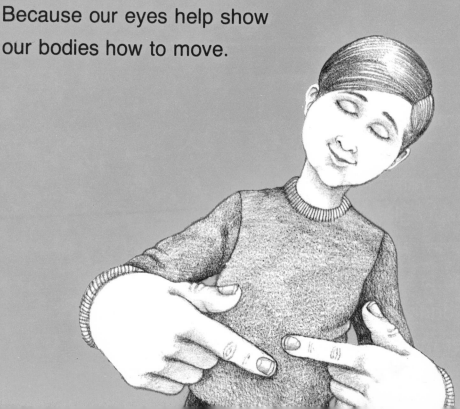

Breathe and Swallow

Breathe through your nose.
Now try to swallow.
Can you do them both
at the same time?
You cannot.
Nobody can.
Your nose and throat are connected
by a little tube in your head.
When you breathe you cannot swallow.
When you swallow you cannot breathe.

Printing Your Name

Can you print your own name?
That's easy!
But sometimes it is very hard.
Look in a mirror.
Try printing your name
while you look in the mirror.
A mirror turns things around.
Try it and you will see!

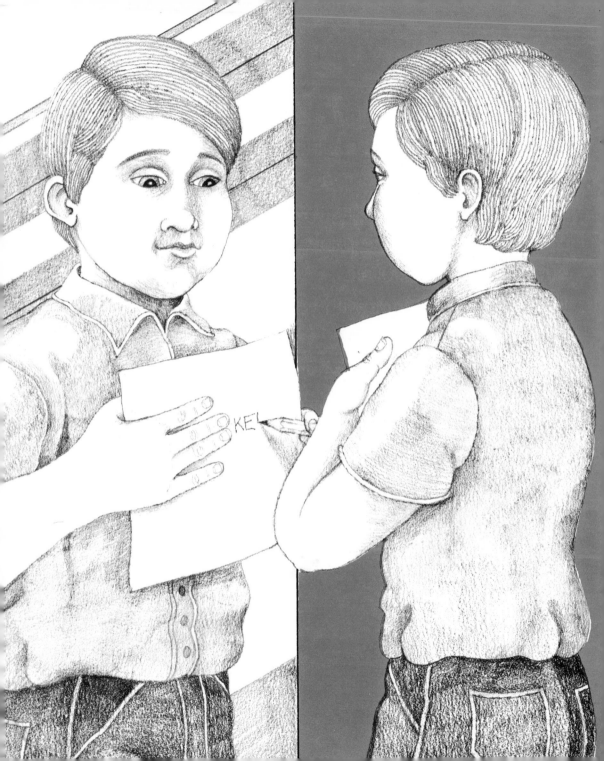

The Blink Game

Roll a sheet of paper into a big ball.
Have a friend look out a window.
You stand on the other side of the window.
Toss the paper ball at his face.
The glass will stop the paper,
but your friend will blink.
Have your friend try it with you.
It is very hard not to blink
no matter how many times you try.

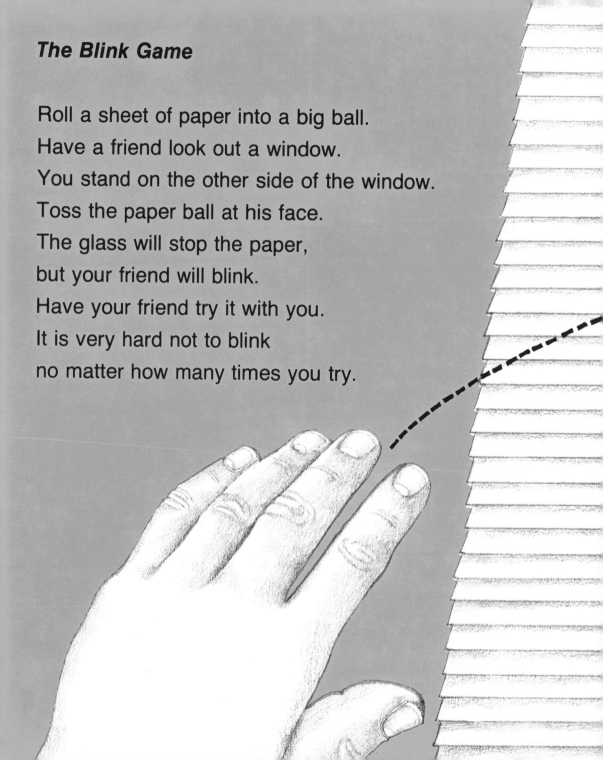

Can You Blow the Ball Out?

Roll a little piece of aluminum foil in a ball.
Drop it in a funnel.
Ask friends to try to blow it out.
They cannot do it.
Their wind goes around the ball,
and out the bottom of the funnel.
Now you blow.
(But, first put your finger over the bottom.)
Now you can blow the ball out.

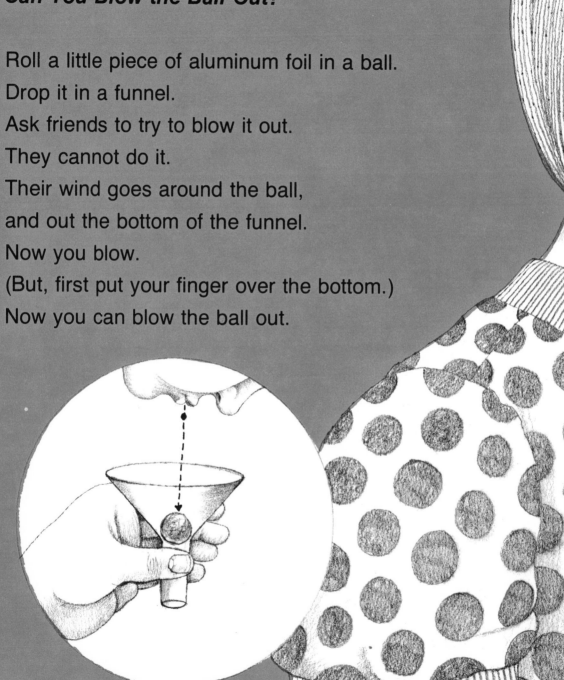

You Can Win This Balance Game

Try to balance a ruler on one finger.
Ask your friends to try too.
It is hard to do.
Who can balance it the longest?
You can!
Try this trick.
Stick a ball of clay on the top of the ruler.
Now try to balance it.
It is much easier now.

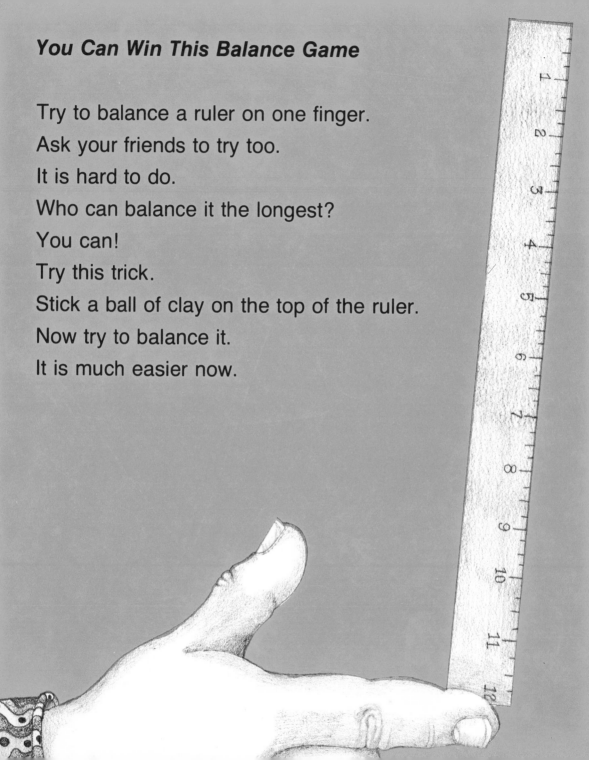

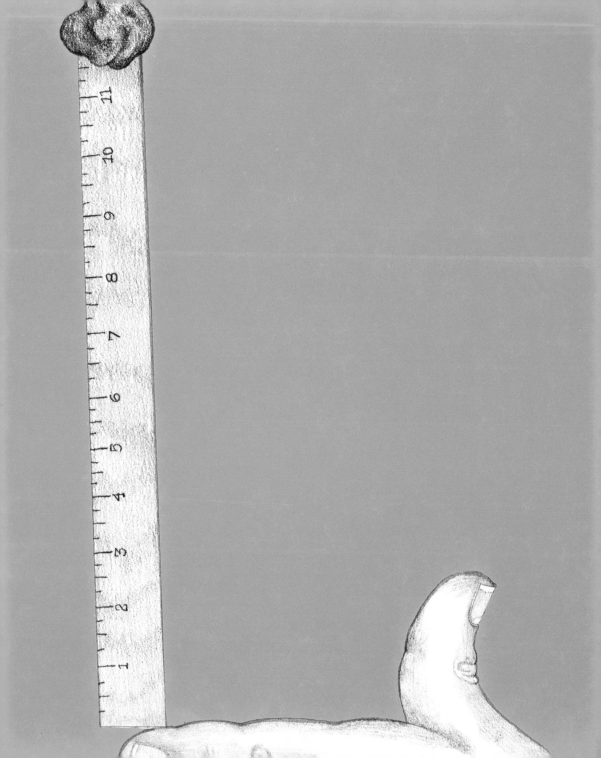

Send Secret Signals

Want to send secret signals to a friend?
And make sure others don't hear the signals?
Have your friend lay his head on a table.
Put your hand under the table.
Tap softly on the bottom of the tabletop.
The sound will travel through the table.
Your friend will hear your secret taps.
But only your friend.
No one else will. Why not?

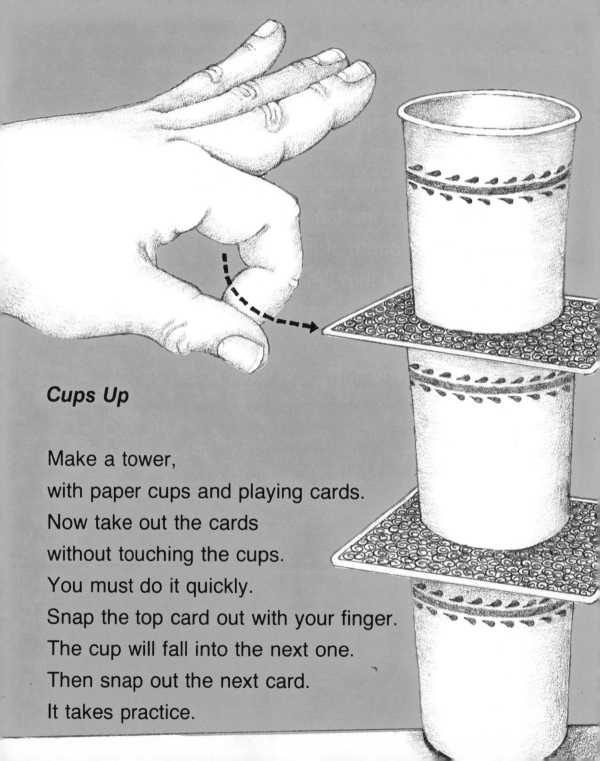

Cups Up

Make a tower,
with paper cups and playing cards.
Now take out the cards
without touching the cups.
You must do it quickly.
Snap the top card out with your finger.
The cup will fall into the next one.
Then snap out the next card.
It takes practice.

Build a Skyscraper

A skyscraper is a tall skinny building.
How high can you build one?
Make it out of paper cups.
Stack them up and down.
The higher . . . the harder!
(I made one eight cups high.)
You cannot make one as tall as a real skyscraper.
But then real skyscrapers are harder to build.

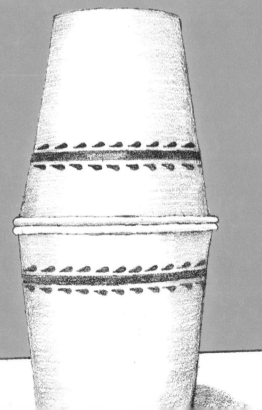

Who Has the Most Teeth?

Count teeth.
Count yours, your friends.'
Babies do not have any teeth at all.
Grown-ups usually have 32 teeth.
You get more teeth as you grow older.
So . . . if you find people with more than you,
do not worry. You will catch up!

WHITE ✪O

TOOTH PASTE OF THE STARS

Is Your Cat Right or Left Pawed?

Some people are right handed.
Some people are left handed.
Which are you?
Which is your cat?
Play a game with your cat and find out.
Put some food in a tall jar.
Put it near your cat.
Which paw does he use to get it out.
Try again.
Does he always use the same paw?

The games in this book work with science.
Like a game, science is something
to try . . .
to learn . . .
and to be good at.
Keep playing these games.

You will get better . . .
And you will understand
more why the games work.
What a nice way
to investigate science.

Puzzles are to Think

A puzzle is a puzzle. . .

. . .only until you know the answer!

A science investigation is a puzzle, too. . .

. . .until you understand it!

This is a book of science puzzles.

Can you. . .

- Freeze a penny in the middle of an ice cube?
- Turn yourself upside down with a teaspoon?
- Eat an apple without tasting it?

Learn the answers. . .

Start investigating!

Can You Count to Twenty?

Watch a friend (maybe a teacher).
Do not tell him what you are doing.
Watch him blink.
Start counting slowly.
One, two, three, four, five . . .
Can you reach 20 before he blinks again?
No! We are always blinking our eyes.
Try to count to 20 and not blink yourself.
Can you do it?

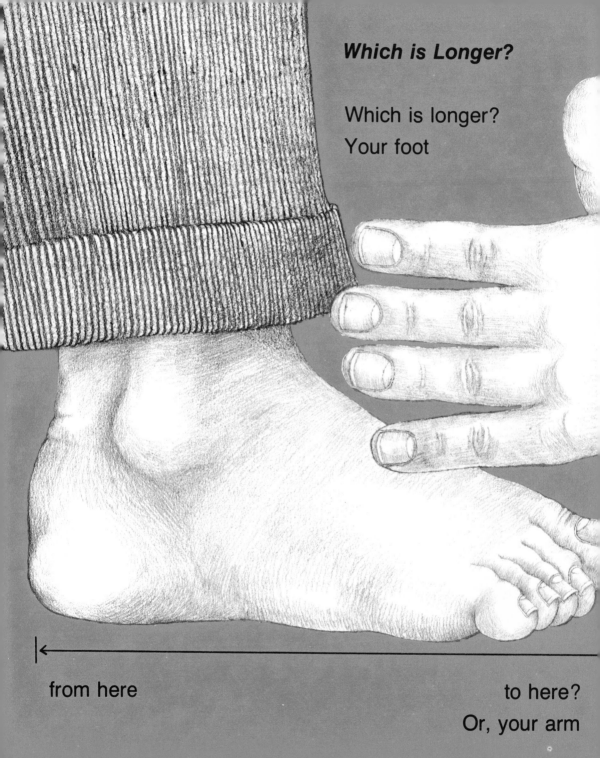

Which is Longer?

Which is longer?
Your foot

from here

to here?
Or, your arm

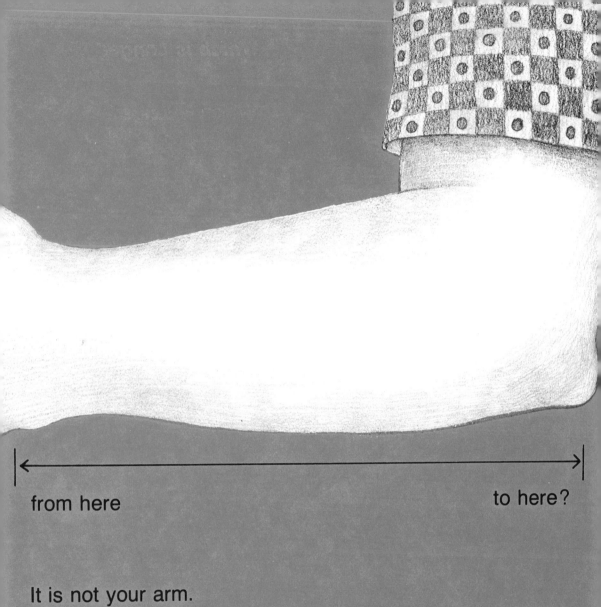

from here   to here?

It is not your arm.

It is not your foot.

They are both about the same length.

Prove it!

Measure them.

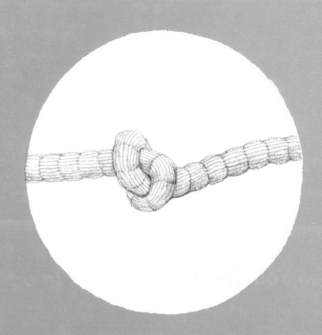

What Happens When You Open Your Arms?

Cross your arms like this.
Hold the ends of a rope tightly in each hand.
Open your arms.
What happens to the rope?
It is tied in a knot.
Why?
You had your arms in a knot.
The knot went over to the rope.

Can You See Yourself Blink in a Mirror?

Look at your eyes in a mirror.
Blink them.
In the mirror, your eyes do not blink.
Why?
The answer is easy.
Shut your eyes.
You cannot see.
You shut your eyes when you blink.
You cannot see the mirror when your
eyes are closed.
Try a one-eyed wink.
Can you see that in a mirror?

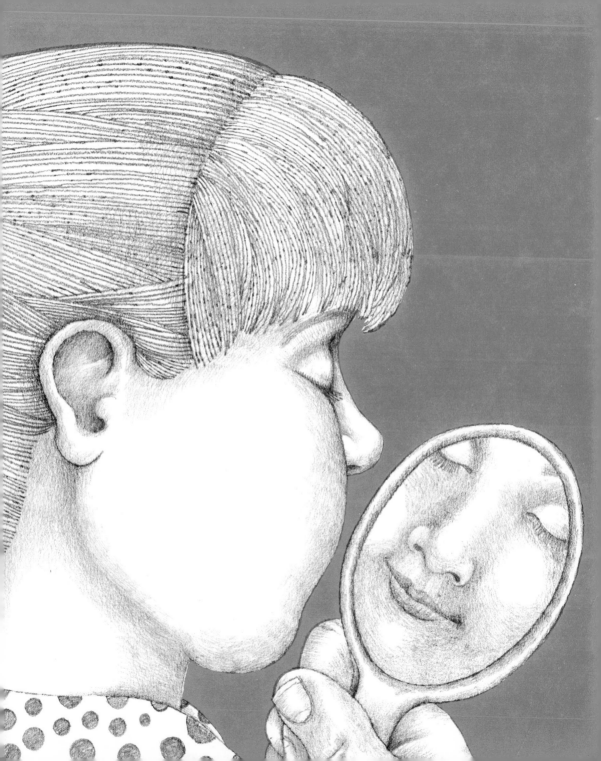

Turn Yourself Upside Down

Look into a mirror.
You see yourself right side up.
Some mirrors turn things upside down.
A spoon is a mirror.
One side curves in.
One side curves out.
If you look at a spoon, you will see yourself.
On one side you will be upside down.
Which side?
Try it.

What Does This Say?

Hold this word to a mirror.

ƎVA◖
◖AVƎ

The mirror turns the word around.
You can write like this.
Print a word on a thin paper.
Turn it over and hold it up to a window.
Copy the letters through the paper.
This is your backwards word.
You can only read it in a mirror.

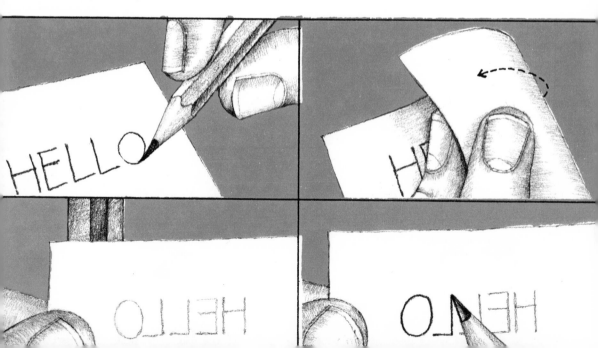

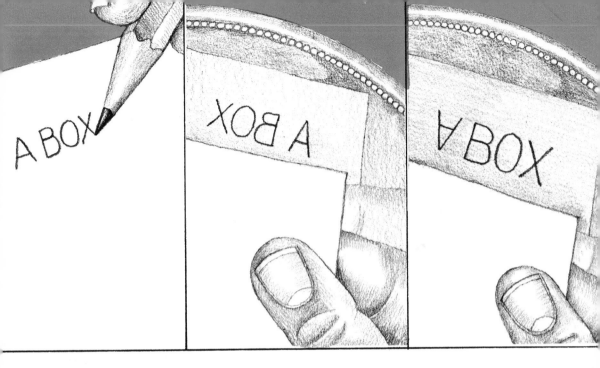

Can a Mirror Fool You?

Print "A BOX" on a piece of paper.

Look at it in a mirror.

While you are looking, turn it upside down.

Look!

"A" is upside down.

But "BOX" is not.

Why?

The letters "B O X" look the same upside down.

The letter "A" looks different upside down.

Whose Footprints are These?

Which set of footprints was made by a person?
They are both people's footprints.

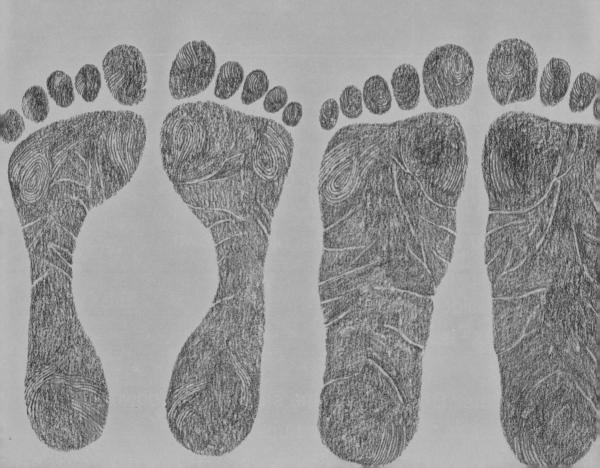

Most people's footprints look like these.
Here the insides of the feet do not touch the floor.

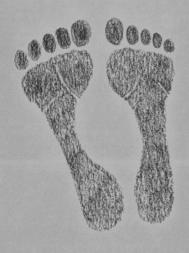

But this person has flat feet.

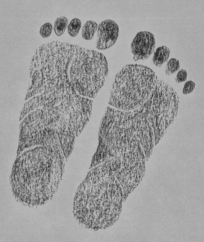

When you take a bath,
Step on the floor with wet feet.
Which set of footprints do you have?
(Be sure to wipe them up!)

Which Hand Feels Colder?

Next time you wash your hands, try this.
Dip both hands in the water.
Hold both hands up.
Which hand feels colder?
They are both the same.
Can you make one colder?
Blow on it.
Wind dries the water.
When the water dries, it makes you cold!

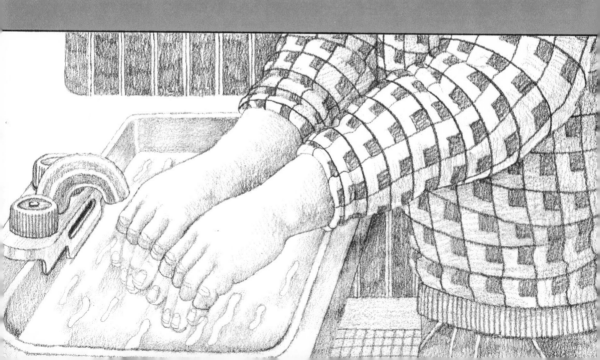

Can You Make Paper Fall Faster?

Hold two sheets of flat paper side by side.
Let them fall together.
Air makes them fall slowly.
Can you make one fall faster?
Roll one sheet into a ball.
Drop the ball and the flat sheet.
The ball drops faster.
The air does not slow it down.

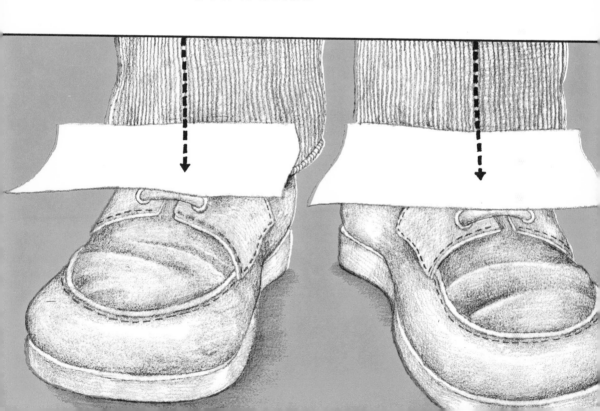

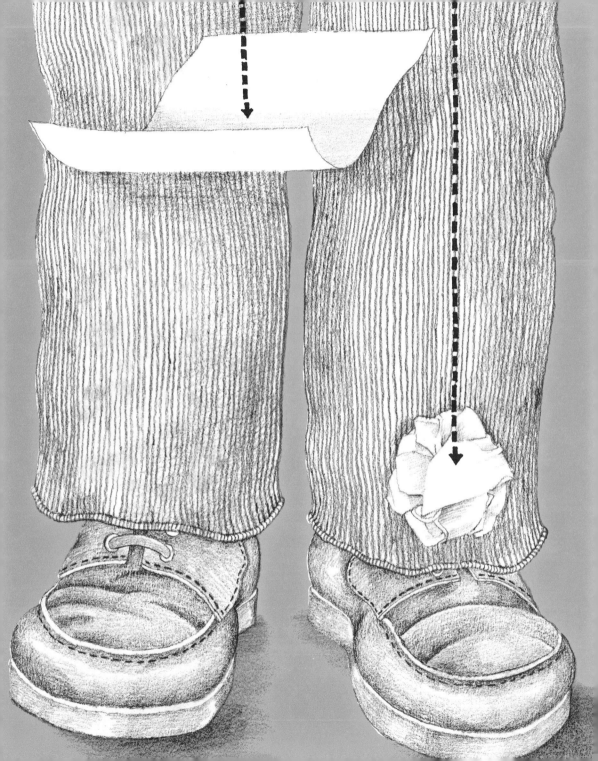

Can You Hear with Your Teeth?

Scratch a pencil with your fingernail.
Can you hear the scratching?
You can hear it just a little.
Hold the pencil in your teeth.
Scratch it.
The scratching noise will be louder.
The noise goes through your teeth,
through your skull,
right to your ears!

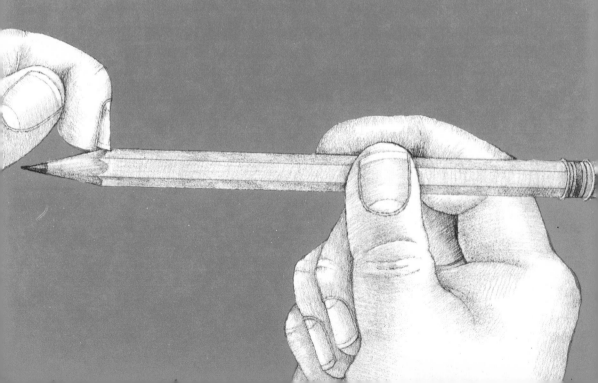

What Holds the Pencil Up?

This looks like a magic trick.

The pencil is not really stuck on the hands.

What holds it up?

Look very carefully.

Most people do not look sharply enough.

Did you?

(Count the number of fingers).

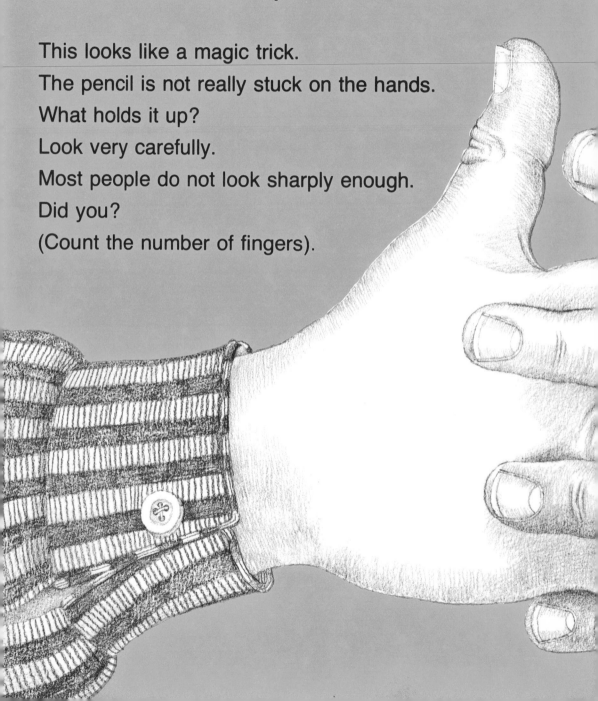

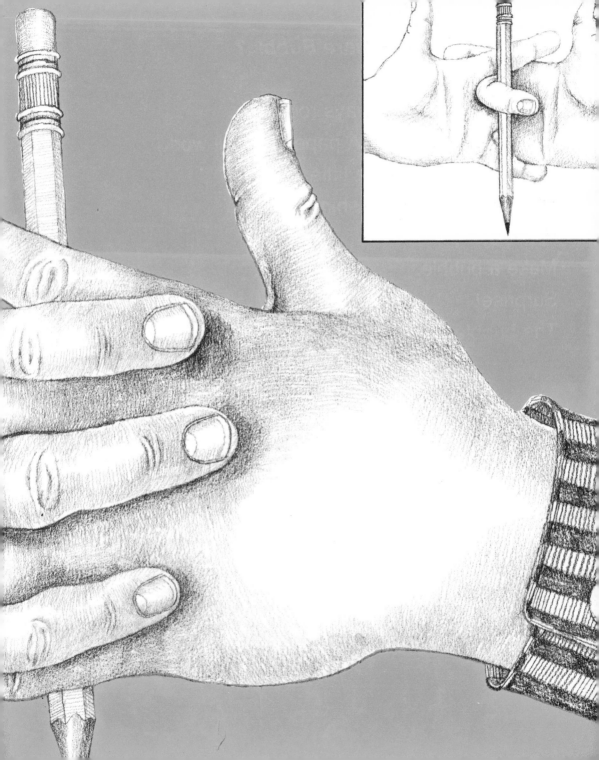

Can You Blow a Square Bubble?

Are soap bubbles always round?

Get a piece of wire. (A paper clip will work).

Bend it square, with a little handle.

Dip it in some dishwashing liquid.

Blow into it.

Make a bubble.

Surprise!

The bubble is round!

Can You Make an Ice Cube with a Penny Inside?

Puzzle your friends with the ice cube.
It has a penny frozen inside.
How?
Fill a paper cup half full of water.
Set it in a freezer until it is frozen.
Put a penny on top of the ice.
Pour some water on top.
Freeze it again.
Tear the cup away from the ice.
The penny is in the ice cube!

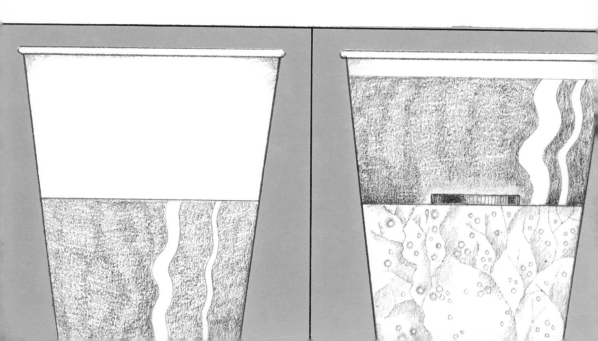

Which Hole Squirts Best?

Do this puzzle over a sink.
Punch three holes in a paper cup.
Use a pencil point.
Fill the cup with water.
The water squirts out the holes.
Which hole squirts best?
The bottom hole squirts best.
The water is deeper.
The deeper water pushes out harder.

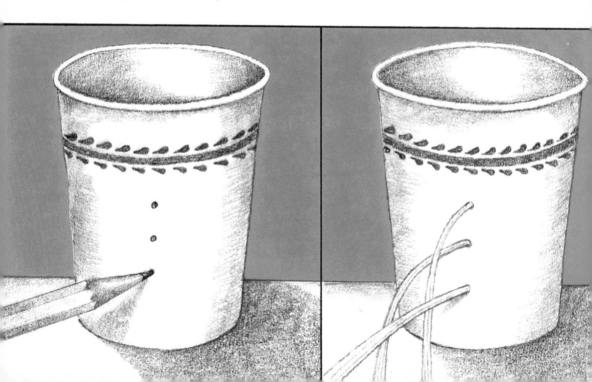

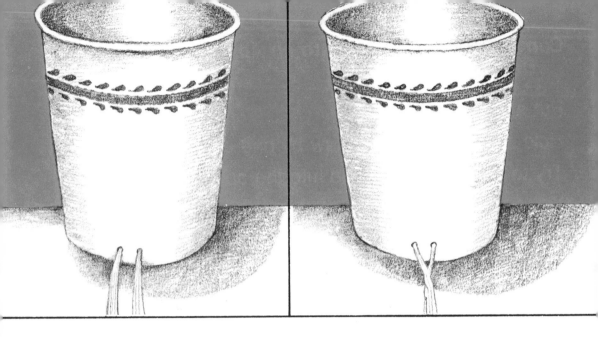

Will Water Stick to Itself?

Poke two small holes in a paper cup.
Make them close together, near the bottom.
Fill the cup with water over a sink.
Two little streams squirt out.
Pinch the two streams together with your fingers.
The two streams stick together!
Break them apart with your fingers.
Pinch them together again.
Water sticks to itself.

Can You Push a Straw Into an Apple?

Put an apple on the table.
Hold a paper drinking straw by one end.
Try to push the other end into the apple.
You cannot.
The apple seems too tough.
But hold a straw above the apple.
Push it down fast.Now the straw is moving quickly.
It does not stop.
It goes right into the apple.

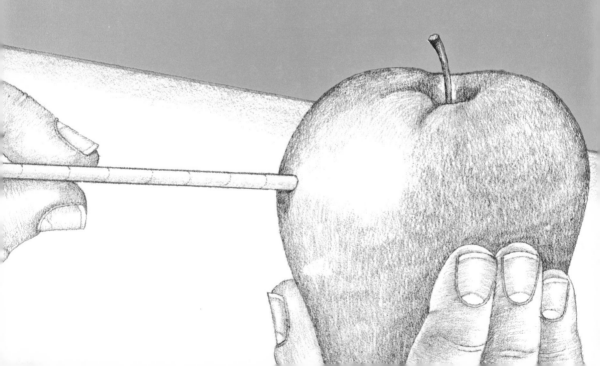

Will They Sink or Float?

Fill a bowl with water.

Drop a raw carrot and an apple into the water.

One will sink.

One will float.

Will the apple float or sink?

Things heavier than water sink.

Things lighter than water float.

The carrot is heavier than water.

Does Your Nose Help You Taste Food?

Get an apple and a potato.

Cut some small pieces of each.

Put them in a paper bag.

Reach in and take a piece out.

Do not look at it.

Hold your nose tightly.

Eat the piece.

Is it an apple or a potato?

You cannot tell.

You cannot taste it.

Your nose does help you taste food.

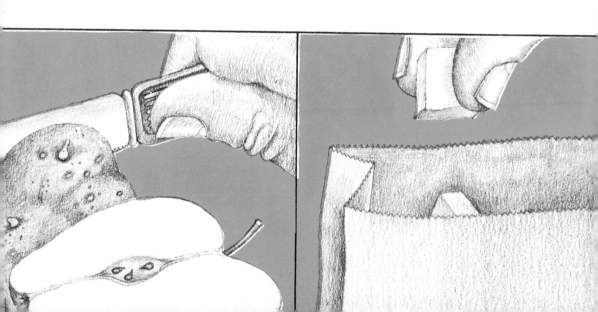

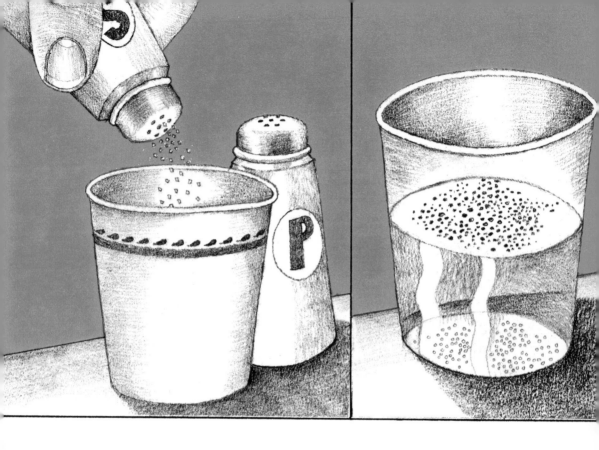

Can You Take Salt and Pepper Apart?

Sprinkle some salt and pepper in an empty paper cup.
Shake the cup to mix them together.
Can you take them apart again?
Pour some water in the cup.
The pepper floats on top.
The salt stays on the bottom.
Salt is heavier than pepper.

Can You Mix These?

Pour a little cooking oil in a clear glass.
Pour in some water.
See what happens?
The water goes down.
The oil floats on top.
Can you mix them together?
Try with a spoon.
After you stir them, wait a minute.
They go apart again.
Some things do not mix.

What Makes a Rainbow?

Do this outdoors in bright sunlight.
Set a clear glass on a piece of white paper.
Fill the glass half full of water.
Tip the glass back and forth.
Look on the paper.
You will see spots of pretty colors.
Sometimes the sun shines on tiny water drops in the sky.
The light turns red, orange, yellow, green, blue and purple.
It is a rainbow!
Your glass makes rainbow colors the same way.

Can You Blow a Book Over?

Set two heavy books close together on a table.
They should stand on their ends.
Can you blow either one over?
No?
You can when you know the trick.
Blow up a balloon between them.
Your breath fills the balloon.
A book falls over.

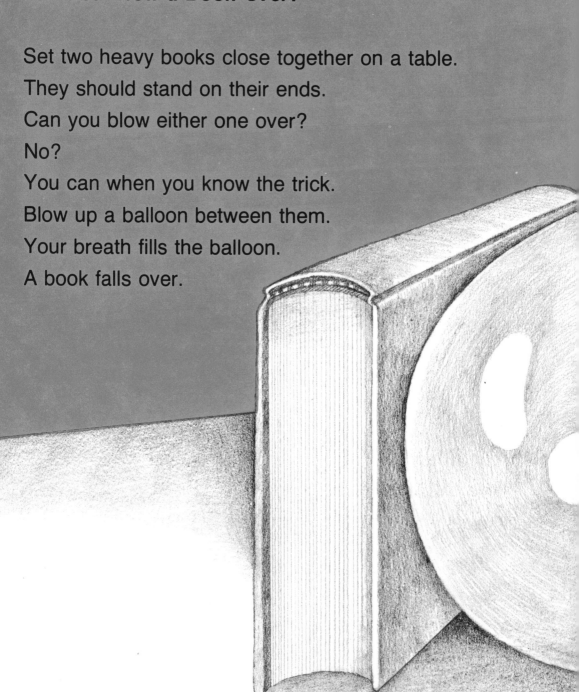

Which Can Will Win?

Take two soup cans, one empty one and one filled with soup
Race them side by side down a hill.
One will always win.
Which one?
The full one!
It is heavier.
It goes faster.

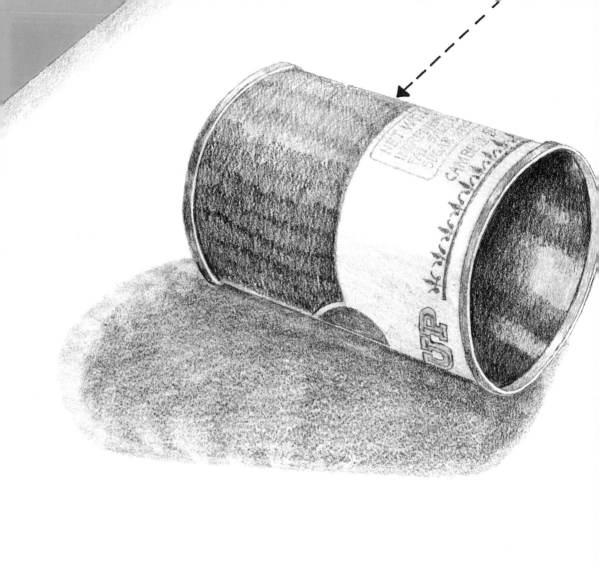

Which Nail Makes the Highest Note?

Nails can make pretty music.

Tie some on a piece of string.

Use different sizes of nails.

Hold the end of the string in your hand.

Tap the nails with another nail.

Each one makes a different musical note.

Do little nails make high or low notes?

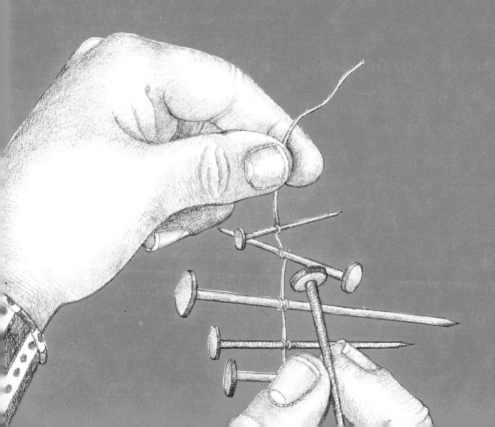

These puzzles are not puzzles any more.

You know the answers.

What can you do now?

Find some science puzzles of your own.

Look around.

Ask questions.

Try things.

Anything you do not understand is just a puzzle looking for an answer.